How to Use Law of Attraction to Win Contests

Written by Steven Scott

Multiple Contest Winner

Disclaimer

This guide was written to explain how I use Law of Attraction to win a contest almost every week. Winning Contests or earning potential is entirely dependent on the person using the techniques. Your level of success in using Law of Attraction to Win Contests depends on the time you devote to the program, ideas and techniques mentioned, knowledge and various skills. There is no guarantee that you will win any contest using this system. This book was written by my personal experience using Law of Attraction to win contests.

Copyright © 2016 Steven R Scott

All rights reserved. No part of this Book may be reproduced or transmitted in any form or by any means, electronic or mechanical, including photocopying, recording or by any information storage and retrieval system, without written permission from the author or publisher.

ISBN-13: 978-1530403103

ISBN-10: 1530403103

How to Use Law of Attraction to Win Contests

Written by Steven Scott

Multiple Contest Winner

This guide was created to help you better understand how to use law of attraction to win contests. I have been following Law of Attraction for the past year and a half, and have been using it to win contests. The past six months, I have won over 30 contests including winning gift cards, vacation trips, jewelry, money, coupons for free items, and much more. I do not win every contest, but I win a lot using Law of Attraction. The system that I use every day is laid out in this guide. Also make sure you do the exercises that are listed in this book. It will help you master my system to winning contests using Law of Attraction. Follow this system and you could become a multiple contest winner.

Winner

**FREE Law of Attraction Newsletter
"IN THE VORTEX"**
*Success Stories, Inspirational Quotes,
Video Clips & Interviews.
Sign up at
InTheVortexNews.com*

Table of Contents

What is Law of Attraction………………………………….…	8
What is a Contest or a Sweepstakes?………………………	10
Reading the Guidelines or Rules ……………………….……	11
My "Discovery" with Law of Attraction……………….……	13
What Do You Want to Win this Year?………………………	19
The First Step………………………………………………...…	23
Where to Find Contests to Enter……………………….……	25
The Second Step………………………………………………	25
Asking the Universe to Win a Specific Contest……………	27
The Third Step…………………………………………………	27
The Power of Affirmations ……………………………….……	29
Visualize Yourself Winning……………………………………	32
How to Create a Vision Board to Win Contests……………	34
Believe that You Won………………………………….…...….	37
The Fourth Step……………………………………………..…	37
Thinking Positive Will Change Your Life……………………	39
Gratitude is Everything……………………………………..…	41
The Fifth Step……………………………………………………	43
The Waiting Game………………………………………………	45
The Sixth Step……………………………………………………	45
Quick Reference Guide …………………………………………	46

Acknowledgements

I would like to thank my wife Tara Scott, who means the world to me. Without her, I wouldn't be the "Lucky" person that I am today. I realize that you had to put up with me entering and also losing contests for years before I started using Law of Attraction and for that I am so ever grateful. Thank you for supporting me for all of the crazy ideas, contests, college, jobs, and everything else that I have done or tried to do in the past. I love you so much!

I must give a shout-out to my three amazing children. Steven, Kevin and Chris, who drive us crazy at times but I love seeing them every day. Watching children grow into early teens can be a challenge. But I truly enjoy the experience.

I would also like to thank my Mother, Luella, who raised my two sisters, brother and I as a single parent. I can't even image how hard or stressful that must have been on you. I know that we have had our differences over the years but I realize that you did the best job that you could have done at the time. So for that, I am very thankful.

I also would like to thank my twin brother, Jim Scott, who did everything with me when we were kids. Even though we are not as close as we once were and live different lives, you're still my brother and I still cherish the time that we do spend together. Going to a Chinese Buffet, or seeing a movie or just hanging out is always fun. Thank you for always being there for me.

I must say EPIC thanks to my sister, Mary Scott Carney. It's been a pleasure having you as my sister. I am sure as a child, I acted "slightly crazy" at times, but I am thankful for having you as one of my sisters. Also I am so glad we got to work together for two years with the EPIC team. I think we worked well together at the hospital!

I would like to thank my sister, Sarah Pineda-Scott, for helping mom take care of us. Thank you for all of the times that our kids came to your home and you gave Tara and I a "kids-free night."

How to Use Law of Attraction to Win Contests

I can't write this book without thanking my mother and father-in-law, Debbie and Jim Shelhamer. You welcomed me into your life when I started dating your daughter. Words can't even begin to express how thankful I am for the love and experiences that we have shared over the years. You have changed my life in so many ways. Debbie, you have always been there to help with our children. Also Jim has helped us countless times with our cars. They were always breaking down and you always came to our rescue with on-the-road assistance. I truly couldn't have asked for better in-laws.

I also wanted to thank my sister-in-law, Kerry Shelhamer, whom I adore and consider my sister. I think you were only 11 or 12 when I first met you and I enjoyed our experiences together: teaching you how to drive, talking about movies, sharing experiences and dreams together. It's been a pleasure seeing you grow up and I know you will go far in life.

I would like to thank "Buckwheat" who was a father figure to me and my siblings growing up. I will always cherish the time you spent with us at the local fire hall, holidays, exciting parades, fishing, and even buying our school supplies and clothes. Words can't even express how much gratitude I have for you.

I also would like to thank my grandmother, "Grammy" who is now in Heaven. She always saw the good in everything and everyone. Her house was always filled with the smell of cookies and love. I'm so glad that my children were able to build a relationship with you too. I love You!

Words can't express how grateful I am to Terri Waskie Gross who agreed to help me edit this guide. I always admired you as a teacher, friend, and somebody that just inspires me to be a better person every day.

I would like to thank the rest of my friends, family, and co-workers and even former co-workers who I have had the privilege to work with. This journey continues to be a great life experience.

I would also like thank all of the people who didn't believe in me, or understand Law of Attraction or thought I was crazy. Guess who else they thought were crazy? Albert Einstein, Abraham Lincoln, Nikola Tesla, Ludwig van Beethoven, Thomas Edison, Andrew Jackson, Werner Heisenberg, etc. Many people that we simply admire or have had a huge impact in our lives (directly or indirectly) at the time others thought their ideas were crazy. Over time, our society has decided to admire them in one way or another.

Most of all, I would like to THANK The Universe and Law of Attraction. Without this force, I would not be able to live the amazing journey that I have accepted. For that, I am very grateful.

Thank

You

Why You Need to Read this book

This book, which you have in your hands, is one of the most powerful Law of Attraction guides that will help you win contests and live a much better life. I have used Law of Attraction in every part of my life for the past year and it has made a huge impact on my life, including winning contests. I am now winning a contest almost every week. I have proven to my friends and family that Law of Attraction works! Law of Attraction is a powerful force that can give you the life you always dreamed of, if you know how to use it. When you understand it, the faster it will manifest your visions into reality. You will learn direct strategies that will help you win contests week after week. You can also manifest more income, less debt, a dream house, the job of your dreams, an exciting new vacation, fewer bills, to be healthier, more friends, and much more.

Law of attraction is being used every day by millions of people. But only a small percentage of people truly use it in every part of their life. This book was created as a guide to help others to understand how to use Law of Attraction to Win Contests.

What is Law of Attraction?

The Law of Attraction is a spiritual belief that can be used by everyone. Law of Attraction is the belief that every positive or negative thing that happens to you was attracted by you. Law of Attraction is the belief that you will experience a certain outcome based on asking the Universe for a specific outcome and then applying your thoughts and feelings and then trusting that the Universe will provide this outcome in your life.

I understand that this may seem like a strange concept to grasp. When I first read about Law of Attraction, I was not 100% behind it either. But then I realized that almost all of us have used Law of Attraction. For example, did you ever really want to work for a certain company or a certain position? So, you imagined yourself working at a certain place, and focused on what you did for that company. Then a month or two goes by and you apply for that job. Then you imagined yourself getting hired, and working for the company. You felt excited to work for them. Within a few weeks, the company calls you for an interview and hires you. Do you remember how great you felt when you found out that you were hired?

Or what about the time that you had a crush on somebody, maybe a co-worker or a friend that you were associated with. So in your mind, you thought about the two of you going out to a nice romantic dinner or maybe seeing a movie. Remember how great you felt when you imagined yourself dating and spending time together. And then a few weeks or months later, you asked the person out and of course the person said yes.

In both these examples, you applied The Law of Attraction without even realizing that you were. Wasn't it exciting when what you imagined became a reality?

Wasn't it exciting when she or he said yes to the first date? I'm sure you have used Law of Attraction in other ways of your life. (Such as a certain car you wanted to buy, or a house, or maybe moving to a certain area)

Are you ready to take full advantage of this life changing power that we have in our minds? Your thoughts and feelings can give you the ability to live the life of your dreams. You can apply Law of Attraction with every area of your life. In this book, I will help guide you to win multiple contests. I have been winning a contest every week for the past six months. I am going to teach you everything that I do to win contests every week.

Thoughts = Reality

What is a Contest or Sweepstakes?

Contests and Sweepstakes are used as a promotion tool to increase the excitement of a brand name, product or service. Every week, hundreds of contests and sweepstakes take place all across the country at local and national grocery stores, restaurants, hotels/resorts, retail stores, manufactures, radio stations, newspapers, TV stations, gas stations, malls, etc. Just about every type of business has offered a contest or sweepstakes as a way to build the excitement around their business.

A sweepstakes will award a winner a prize based on a random draw. Winners are selected based on chance. A contest is designed to be more interactive with the people that enter. This can include having to upload a photo, video, or some kind of essay that is attached to the entry. Winners are usually selected based on the rules of the contests such as creativity and stand out from the other entries.

Imagine yourself winning contests every week or even every month. Can you image even winning a big contest a few times per year? I have been winning a contest every week. I use the same method every contest that I enter. In this guide, I will be teaching you how to win any contest you want to win.

Reading the Guidelines or Rules

Before you enter a contest or sweepstakes you always want to spend a few minutes reading the guidelines or the rules. You will learn more information about the giveaway such as the start and the end, how many times you can enter, and what they are looking for when they select a winner. If it's a sweepstakes that wants you to upload a photo or video, you must make sure you follow the guidelines/rules. For example, I entered a sweepstakes where it wanted me to take a picture of myself with the product but it couldn't show any logos of other companies in the picture. Now, can you image if I entered a few pictures wearing a shirt that had a logo of a different company across the front? My entry would have been disqualified. Also some contests and sweepstakes will limit you on how many times you may enter. It might just be a limit of once per day or maybe only one time for the entire contest or sweepstakes.

It is very important to spend a few minutes before you enter a contest or sweepstakes to review the guidelines or rules. I have entered a few contests and sweepstakes in the past and didn't realize that they had a limit such as one entry per contest, and I was disqualified.

How to Use Law of Attraction to Win Contests

I have won many contests and sweepstakes using Law of Attraction. This method will work for both. In this book, I will be referring to both contests and sweepstakes as just contests. It's the same method regardless if you are entering a contest or a sweepstakes.

I hope you are excited to learn this system and to start winning contests!

Enjoy Winning Contests

FREE Law of Attraction Newsletter
"IN THE VORTEX"
Success Stories, Inspirational Quotes, Video Clips & Interviews.
Sign up at
InTheVortexNews.com

My "Discovery" with Law of Attraction

About a year ago, I was in a much different place. We lived in a small town in Northeast PA. Businesses seemed to always be closing. Local companies were either laying off or not hiring anybody. About every other week we read about another household getting busted for a Meth Lab. My wife, three kids, and I were living in an older house that needed work done. This includes a new furnace, windows, roof, flooring, etc. I was laid off from my job again, and collecting unemployment. My wife was also getting treated for cancer for the second time in three years. Life was very depressing and dark. We were facing some really hard times. We were living off credit cards and didn't understand why nothing seemed to be working out.

Now I must admit to you. I am usually a positive person. I have read several books on positive thinking over the last few years, and tried to look at the positive side of what we were going through. I didn't understand why we were living like this when so many people are living a much better life. I didn't understand why I couldn't get a decent steady job, after all, I did have a Master's Degree in Business. I didn't understand how to turn it around. Seeing my wife face cancer for the second time in three years, really opened my eyes. It made me think about everything: our life together, jobs, kids, etc. I knew in my heart that there had to be a better way. How do other people live a much better life and we were at the bottom?

I started looking for answers. I was laid off at the time, so I started looking online and at books for maybe something I could try to do. I always believed in the concept of thinking positive but I knew there had to be something more. With my weeks of research, I discovered The Law of Attraction. I started using it every day (I will talk about this in more details soon). This included my use of a vision board.

A few weeks went by and my wife was back to work and everything seemed back to "normal." We decided to take a weekend trip to Hershey Park (without the kids) as a way to "celebrate" that my wife was doing ok with her health issues.

We went to Hershey Park and had such an exciting time: did the Hershey Trolley Tour, ate at a few restaurants etc. It was a perfect weekend getaway. Something we both needed! The weather was great and the area was amazing. I picked up a newspaper and saw tons of places hiring in this area.

As we drove home (about 1.5 hours away) we were smiling and talking about how what a great weekend we had together. She agreed that this is what we needed. I casually said to her, wouldn't it be great to live in Hershey or in this area?

She of course agreed. It was so close to several outlets, malls, tons of restaurants and everything you could possibly want to do.

After I got home, I added it to my vision board. I posted that we would move to the Hershey area. I imagined it over and over again how much fun it would be to live so close to Hershey Park, and how exciting it would be to have a decent job and what our apartment would look like. I imagined it would have a swimming pool, basketball court, be in an apartment complex. I was so excited that it didn't seem like a vision. It was fun to imagine what it would be like to live in this reality. I imagined this in my head over and over for two weeks.

How to Use Law of Attraction to Win Contests

About two weeks went by, and I received a letter from the Unemployment Office stating that I can only collect for one more week. I was so scared and nervous. I had no idea what I was going to do. At the time, I had applied for several jobs without much luck. Plus, I didn't apply for many when my wife was getting treated for cancer and now I am going to face no income. I had worked at an Amazon warehouse before and I knew they would hire me. I went down and applied. They offered me the position right away. I didn't want to go back to working at a warehouse like I did years ago. I didn't want to go back to that life again. My wife came home from work and I explained to her that my unemployment was done and that I will have to work at a warehouse until I can get something else. We were both frustrated with life, but I knew I didn't have a choice at the time. I had to support my wife and family.

I didn't understand why Law of Attraction wasn't working. But it didn't stop me from trying at the time. Over and over I imagined how different my life can be in that area.

Within a few days, one of the jobs that I applied for called me for an interview. It was Hershey Foods in Hershey PA. I was shocked and excited. It was for the sales dept. I was so excited I couldn't believe that maybe everything was going to happen. After I set up the interview I went on craigslist and found a room to rent. I figured maybe I can move down and work and then have my wife and kids move down by the end of summer. This was happening so fast I couldn't have been more excited.

The day that I had my interview, the temp service called me again. So I finally called them back and told them that I was moving to the Hershey area and to take me off their list. They said they had open positions in Camp Hill which is in that area. I explained to them that I had an interview with Hershey but I am open to that position if I don't get the other job. A few hours after my Hershey interview, I got the call that nobody likes. I didn't get the job. I called the temp service back and told them that I was interested. They hired me over the phone and I started Monday. This was Friday. My wife came home Friday after working all day. I told her that I didn't get the Hershey job but the temp service has a job for me starting Monday in Camp Hill, and that I found a room for rent that was very affordable. We both were in shock but knew in our hearts that it will bring us to this area and a better life. This was the first time that Law of Attraction worked for me. It was also the same time I realized that I now hold the power to changing my reality by my thoughts.

Within a year, I was using Law of Attraction (LOA) for everything in my life.

Including:

Dream Apartment

Our apartment – I imagined it will be in an apartment complex with a swimming pool, and basketball court.

LOA – We found an apartment complex that was within our budget with a swimming pool, basketball court. It was only a few minutes from where I rented a room. We found it just by driving around.

Student Loans

No Student Loans – I imagined not having to make any more student loans. I have my Master's Degree in Business and have about $47,000 in student loans. At the time, I was paying around $300 per month.

LOA – I received a letter in the mail that I may qualify for student loan forgiveness based on income and size of house. To get approved, I had to fill out several papers, proof of income, size of house, etc. Guess how much my payment will now be? "$0" Based on our household size and income. We love not having to make that student loan payment every month!

How to Use Law of Attraction to Win Contests

Dream Job

Teaching Job – The past three years I was working for a temp service offering software support to hospitals. Because it was a temp job, I was getting laid off for months every year. I always wanted to teach at a college. I thought it would be fun. I thought the possibility of teaching computers or business would be exciting. I imagined myself helping students and having weekends and holidays off. I imagined myself working for 2 colleges, and an online college. Granted, I had never taught at a college before.

LOA – It was around Sept of 2015 when I got an email from a Business & Technical College. They wanted me to come down for an interview. After about 30 minutes, they offered me the job to teach part time. I was excited. The next day, I went online and found they had a closer campus from my house. So I went in and talked to them. They wanted me to teach part time for them in computers. I didn't have any experience in teaching, and I now had two colleges that wanted me to teach computers part time. A few days later, an online college asked me to teach a class online. Wow, I couldn't believe it, everything I imaged came to my reality!

Win Multiple Contests

Contests – So I have to admit to you. I love contests. I have been entering contests for years without winning much. I would win a contest every year or so at the most. I started imagining myself winning multiple contests. This includes new vehicles, gift cards, trips to a Tropical Island, Las Vegas, Disney, etc. I felt like it would be so amazing to win prizes every week.

LOA – The past six months I have been winning a contest almost every week. This includes free vacation trips, gift cards to local, national and online stores, gift certificates to several restaurants, concert tickets, movies, and much more. I have won as many as four contests in a week and I have gone a few weeks without winning anything.

I must say, it's exciting to get an email or a phone call saying that I won!!! It didn't cost me a penny to enter, just a few minutes of my time. I have to admit; I don't win every contest. Wouldn't it be amazing to win even a few contests every year? Or what about if you could win a contest every few months? By using Law of Attraction, I have proven it every week that it can be done. I have been winning a contest almost every week since January. Follow this guide and you will be on your way to winning more contests.

Winning contests has nothing to do with Luck. It has all to do with Law of Attraction. And this guide will teach you how to apply Law of Attraction to Win Contests.

Win More Contests

How to Use Law of Attraction to Win Contests

What Would You Like to Win this Year?

House

What does the house of your dreams look like? Wouldn't it be nice to win a nice three or four-bedroom house in the country with a white picket fence? Or what about a new exotic beach house next to the ocean? Or how about a luxury condo on top of a high end building in the city?

Vacation

Wouldn't it be amazing to go on a free vacation like a romantic getaway to an island such as the Virgin Islands or what about checking out Paris? Wouldn't it be wonderful to walk around the island and visit the little shops in town, and enjoy activities such as scuba diving, taking long walks along the beach, or enjoying a romantic dinner on the beach?

When was the last time you went on a family vacation? Wouldn't it be exciting for your family to win a trip that included plane tickets, hotel, theme park tickets, and gift cards to spend? When was the last time you went on a family vacation that didn't cost you a penny?

Car

What is the sports car of your dreams? Want to win a fast little sports car that you always wanted to own but never really could afford to buy? Wouldn't it be exciting to not only own a fast little sports car, but receive it for free due to a contest giveaway? (ok maybe sales tax and income tax based on your state's current laws)

Wouldn't it be great to win a new minivan for your family or a new SUV? How many years have you had the family car or van? I'll bet you the mileage is getting pretty high. How does winning a new family minivan with only a few hundred miles or less on it sound? Maybe something brand new, that has built in Satellite radio, TVs, and designed with multiple air bags for your children's safety. And guess what? You can win this for your family. Can you imagine how excited your children are going to be in this new family minivan or SUV?

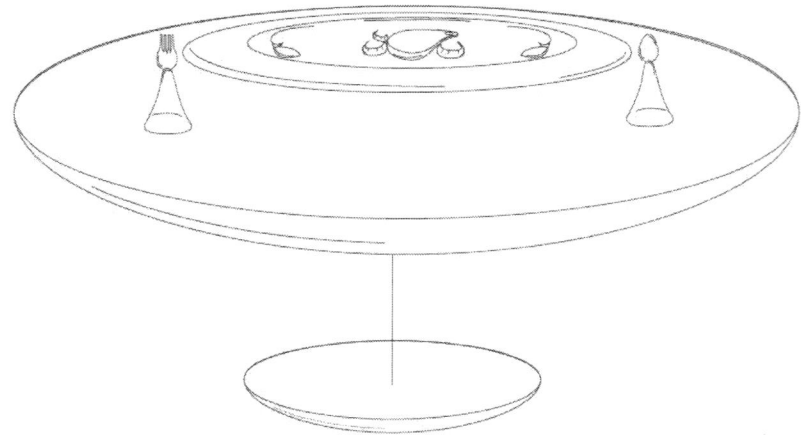

Dine Out

Do you love going out to eat? Most of us do. For one thing, it's less work on our part. Who really wants to work all day and then come home and cook a dinner for your family after working all day? Wouldn't it be great to win gift cards to local restaurants? I love going to restaurants with my family. But I love the idea of not having to pay for it by using a gift card. Wouldn't it be amazing to take your family to a nice five-star restaurant, maybe a Chinese restaurant, or even a fast food place without having to pay for it with your own money? Imagine paying for your order with a gift card that you won.

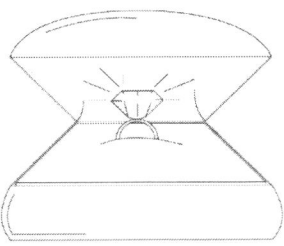

Jewelry

When was the last time you bought your significant other jewelry? Perhaps a new ring, or necklace, or even a nice watch. Image how surprised they will be when you give it to them, and then you later (much later) tell them that you won it from a contest (or maybe don't tell them). How about a shopping spree?

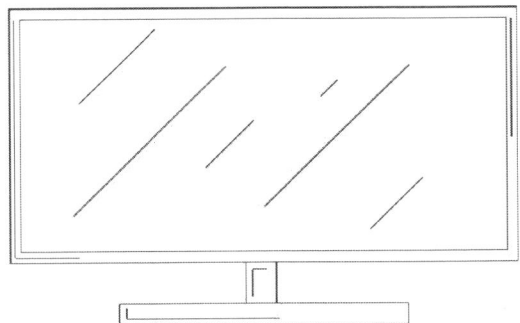

Electronics

Perhaps you would like to start winning electronics. Imagine winning flat screen TVs, computers, stereos, etc. It's fun to replace electronics with new state-of-the-art features without having to pay for it.

How to Use Law of Attraction to Win Contests

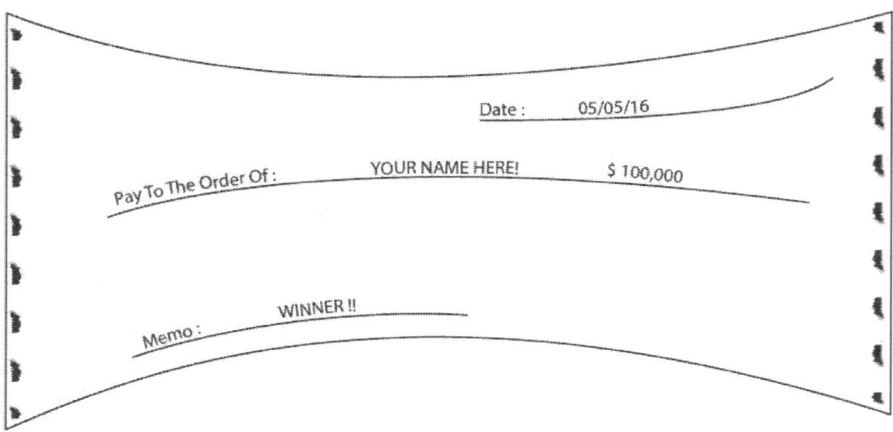

Extra cash to spend

Image checking your mailbox and seeing a check in the mail for $100,000. How would $100,000 change your life? You can now afford to pay off your credit card debt or college loans. Or maybe pay off a past due or current loan. Maybe add on to your house or maybe pay off your house. Can you imagine receiving a $300,000 check in the mail or even a million dollars? Just image how different your life would be if you received a check in the mail for a million dollars. Maybe you can quit your second job, or maybe spend more time with your family by only working part time or maybe even an early retirement. How great would it be to work somewhere because you love doing it and not for the money or the benefits because you won a contest?

Wouldn't it be fun and exciting to win a contest every week or even every month?

Win Cash

Do You Believe in Luck?

Did you ever notice that some people win contests all the time while most people do not? Do you think its luck? Or do you think they are possibly doing something else that nobody else knows about. I thought for years that some people were just born with more luck than others. This is how I felt until I discovered that I can win contests using Law of Attraction.

I am going to share with you, in this guide, my secrets to winning multiple contests. I have been winning a contest almost every week and I want to share with you my secret to winning. It has nothing to do with luck. I use Law of Attraction to Win Contests.

The First Step

The first step of How to Use Law of Attraction to Win Contests is deciding on what you would like to win. Do you want to win a flat screen TV, maybe a new computer, how about new bedroom furniture or maybe even just a gift card? Sometimes I see a contest before I know that I want to win it. If you put enough energy into winning a contest, it will work either way. I have won contests both ways. I would highly suggest on focusing on smaller contests at first to help build up your confidence to win. It doesn't matter how small or large the prize is, it's the same process.

What Do You Want To Win?

Exercise 1

What would you like to win this month?

_____

_____

_____

What would you like to win within six months?

_____

_____

_____

What would you like to win within one year?

_____

_____

_____

What would you like to win within five years?

_____

_____

_____

Where to Find Contests to Enter

Now that you know what you want to win, the next step is finding a contest that is offering that giveaway. I am so grateful that we live in a time where we can search for something online within seconds. The easiest way for me to find a contest is to just go online and search for it.

For example, if I wanted to win a trip to Las Vegas, I would just simply search the internet by typing:

Win a Las Vegas Vacation

Win a trip to Vegas

Enter Las Vegas Trip

I would say almost every contest that I entered; I found it by searching for it online. Now, granted, I have entered and won contests on the local radio station and at local businesses. But with the power of the internet, I have entered contests from companies that I have never heard of only because I found it online. Take a few minutes and search for a few contests.

The Second Step

The second step of How to Use Law of Attraction to Win Contests is to enter the contest. After you decide on what you want to win, next you will need to enter the contest. Make sure you review and follow the guidelines and rules.

Exercise 2

Go to the internet and search for websites that list multiple contest giveaways.

List all of the websites that offer contests lists. (This will help you when you want to refer back to enter more contests in the near future)

_____

_____

_____

_____

_____

_____

_____

_____

_____

_____

_____

_____

_____

Asking the Universe to Win a Specific Contest

I believe that you need to put the message out to the Universe that you want to win a specific contest. Did you ever want something to happen and said it out loud or to yourself that you want or need to make this happen? And then most of the time, it became part of your reality? This is the same process. You need to ask the Universe to win the contest. The Universe needs to know that you want to win a specific contest or prize.

The Third Step

The third step of How to Use Law of Attraction to Win Contests is to ask the Universe to win a specific contest. By asking the Universe to win a contest, you are putting the message out to the Universe that you would like to win. The Universe is always listening to our desires.

Ask The Universe

Exercise 3

I believe you have to ask the Universe to win a specific contest. When I do this, I usually try to focus more on one contest at a time and I try to be as detailed as possible. I have asked for multiple prizes but I find it best to concentrate on one specific contest at a time.

Example: "Universe I want to win a trip to Las Vegas that ABCD Company is giving away."

Practice asking the Universe for a contest you want to win

"Universe I want to win…

_____

_____

_____

_____

_____

_____

_____

_____

_____

_____

_____

The Power of Positive Affirmations

What are affirmations? Affirmations are positive statements that are desired and are often repeated over and over until they are in our subconscious. This process influences the subconscious mind to work on the desired outcome to become true. When you repeat positive statements or thoughts over and over your subconscious mind will accept it as a true statement and you will attract it to your life.

This also works true with negative words or thoughts. Words and thoughts can be used to either build or destroy us. It's how we use them to bring positive or negative experiences. Your subconscious mind will accept what you are saying or thinking about.

For example, if you are doing something that is new, you need to repeat positive affirmations to help you overcome this new challenge.

Using words such as

I am the winner

I am ready to receive a large amount of money

I am grateful to win the contest I entered

I am ready to win multiple contests this year

I deserve to win

If you ever lose your confidence to win contests, please review the positive affirmations in this book.

I Am The Winner

How to Use Law of Attraction to Win Contests

To use the Law of Attraction to Win Contests you will have to become a master at the power of positive affirmation and decide in your mind that you will win something before it will happen. This is the most challenging part of using Law of Attraction to Win Contests. It was a challenge for me to think that I had already won a contest before a winner was selected. I had to believe in my mind that I had already won the contest and that it was lined up for me. This will become easier and easier over time. When you start winning contests, it will get easier and easier to believe you won it before you did.

I entered at least 10 different contests per year for the past 15 years without much luck. I would see a contest, get excited, then enter. But part of me didn't think I would win. I didn't think I would win due to my lack of winning over the past 15 years. I believe lottery players run into the same issue. I believe my negative thoughts were influencing my failure at winning contests. It wasn't until I started using positive affirmations that the doors to me for winning contests opened.

I have won over 30 contests within the first six months of 2016. I started winning contests every week. About two weeks before I won my first contest this year, I repeated to myself over and over a few times per day that I won this drawing, and that the Universe had it lined up. I started believing that I won. I felt excited. I also felt slightly emotional when I received the gift card in my mind. When I received an email stating that I won the gift card, I was excited because I then realized that I can win contests every week using Law of Attraction.

Because I have won so many contests, I believe that it is easier for me to know that I will win a contest. But after you start winning contests, you will soon see how easy it is to believe that you will win before they contact you with the prize.

Exercise 4

List positive affirmations that you will win contests

Example "I am a contest winner"

_____

_____

_____

_____

_____

_____

_____

_____

_____

_____

_____

_____

_____

Visualize Yourself Winning

To win a contest using Law of Attraction, you have to visualize yourself winning. I usually visualize myself winning a contest a few times before I win. For example, I entered (and won) a $100 gift card to a local restaurant a few months ago. I visualized the company emailing me stating that I was the winner of the contest. Then I imagined receiving it in the mail and showing the winning ticket to my wife and kids. I imagined all of us going out to eat, ordering our food, and sitting down, and all enjoying a family night out together. While I imagined this in my mind, I felt very excited and proud that I was able to win this gift card and used it for my family. After I visualized this, I felt like it had already happened. I felt very happy. The next morning, I checked my email, and realized that I actually did win the prize!

The Law of Attraction reacts to thoughts and emotions. It doesn't understand words. When I visualize myself winning a contest, I will try to be as detailed as possible. I usually try to imagine sound, sight, taste, and emotion. Also you have to focus on the feelings. Because the Universe will respond to your thoughts and feelings.

I entered a contest to win a one week stay at a St. Thomas resort. I imagined being excited when I received an email that I won.

How to Use Law of Attraction to Win Contests

I imagined us walking down to the ocean holding hands and enjoying the feeling of the warm sand on our feet, the sounds of the ocean waves, seeing our children playing in the distance, and then I imagined us enjoying a nice dinner at a local bar and grill next to the resort. Soon, I received confirmation of my winning the contest!

If you enter a contest, visualize yourself winning, then imagine the excitement when you receive the prize. For example, I won a gift card to an online Jewelry store for my wife. I imagined winning the contest. Then I imagined having her go online to pick it out. When it came to our house, I imagined myself putting the new necklace on her neck and going out on a nice dinner together. When we went out, she saw a few coworkers who told her how nice her necklace was and she told them that I won it from an online contest. I imagined her being very thankful and me being excited that she was wearing it all night.

The following week I won the jewelry gift card. Now if you look at this example, I only spent a few seconds of my time imagining that I won. Most of the thought was the feelings that I received by giving it to her, and us going out and everyone saying how great it looked.

When I started visualizing winning, I realized very quickly that it was more exciting to imagine myself enjoying the prize than just imagining being the contest winner.

For example, if you wanted to win a car that the local car dealership was giving away, you don't want to just focus on them handing you a check for $25,000 for a new car. You want to visualize yourself winning a car. Then driving the car off the lot, maybe picking up your spouse or a friend, and the feeling you get when everyone looks at you driving the car around town. Also imagine maybe having the radio on, the smell of the new car, maybe your friend or family saying how lucky you are, maybe even taking your friends or family to a drive- thru restaurant and enjoying the new car together. The easiest way to visualize yourself winning is using a vision board.

How to Create a Vision Board to Win Contests

Have you ever heard of the term vision board? A vision board is a tool used to focus on a specific outcome or goal. A vision board displays images or text on a board that represents what you want to receive or accomplish.

Vision boards help you:

1. Reinforce your intentions

2. Focus on your daily affirmation

3. Display specific outcomes more clearly

I usually have multiple vision boards at any given time for several contests. I also use a vision board for specific life goals.

What is the easiest way to create a vision board?

The easiest way for me to create a vision board is using any word processing document. I will start a blank document and then do an online search of images that represents to me what I want to win. Then copy and paste the images onto a blank document. You can also include typed words if you need something specific that you can't find an image of.

My First Vison Board

I created my first vision board about a year ago when I first started using Law of Attraction for some of the things I wanted in my life.

My first vision board showed me moving to the Hershey area, owning a new Jeep, becoming a college instructor, taking a few trips that I wanted to experience: such as going to Disney with my family and going to Las Vegas with my brother. Within two weeks from creating my vision board I had accepted a temp job in the Hershey area. When I started using them to win contests, I realized the contests that I was winning were usually the ones that I created on a vision board. Vision boards are a great tool because it forces your mind to be more detailed about your visions. I am always updating my vision board. I am always creating new vision boards for new contests that I am entering.

For some of the larger contests, I will use a vision board for just one specific contest. For example, if I want to win a trip to Las Vegas, I will start a blank word processing document. Then I will search for several items that remind me of Las Vegas. For example, the famous Las Vegas logo, a few of the casino resorts, maybe some of the shows, restaurants, or an image of a plane, hotel, etc. I try to be as detailed as possible because it helps me when I envision winning the trip.

I have won contests without using a vision board. Using a vision board helps because it helps you create a more detailed vision of winning a specific contest. I usually don't use them for smaller contests, but I use them all the time for larger contests. It helps when I image myself winning the contest, because it helps me visualize more details about winning the contest.

You will want to create a vision board to help you stay focused on something specific that you want to win. I usually look at my vision board(s) a few times per day for a few weeks before a contest. It also keeps me focused on what I am going to win soon. When you are looking at the vision board, focus on how it feels when you win or receive it. For example, if you wanted to win a vacation trip, you want to focus on visualizing on what you are going to do and how it feels. Try to be very detailed when you are visualizing something. Focus on your emotions. Concentrate on the feelings of excitement or joy of it.

Exercise 5

In this exercise you will create your own vision board. This will be fun. Open a word processing program. Then you want to go on to the internet and search for images related to the contest that you want to win.

In this exercise, I want you to create a sample vision board to focus on winning a trip to Las Vegas. Let's say you want to win a vacation to Las Vegas. Search for Las Vegas images.

Search for images for each category and copy and paste it

1. Search for an image of an airplane (since you most likely will be flying to Las Vegas)
2. Search for an image of a hotel/resort where you would like to stay (Maybe something on the strip close to all of the casinos)
3. Search for a few images of some of the casinos you want to visit
4. Search for some restaurants/dance clubs/bars that you want to check out
5. Search for other main attractions
6. Search for the Las Vegas logo (it's very famous)
7. Search for images that say WIN, CONTEST, LAS VEGAS

After you copy and pasted all of the Las Vegas images onto the word processing document, simply just print it out. Congratulations, you have just completed your first vision board.

Believe that You Won

This might be the most challenging part of winning contests using Law of Attraction. You have to believe that you won the contest before they announce the winner. This step is very critical because when you believe that you already won the contest, the Universe will line it up for you. Did you ever really want a job? When they called you for that interview, did you ever 100% believe that it was lined up for you or that you will get hired before you knew they would hire you? Then the company called you to offer you the position. This is the same process. You have to believe 100% that you will win the contest before you know if you won. Sometimes when I enter a contest, I will not win and I realize later that it was because I didn't 100% believe that I was going to win. You need to believe in it with all of your heart. And you will win.

The Fourth Step

The fourth step of How to Use Law of Attraction to Win Contests is to believe that you will win the contest before you win it. Visualize yourself winning a contest. Try to believe every detail and put emotions into your thoughts. Try to spend at least a few minutes for each time you are visualizing yourself winning a specific contest. I would recommend doing it a few times to help you believe that its lined up for you to win.

Believe

Exercise 6

Let's practice visualizing winning a $500 gift card. This will be fun. Imagine yourself entering a contest to win $500. You just received a phone call or email that you are the grand prize winner. How are you going to spend the extra $500? Try to be very detailed and specific.

When I win the $500 gift card I am going to spend it on….

Thinking Positive Will Change Your Life

Have you ever had a positive day? You wake up to birds chirping and felt very grateful for the sounds. Your spouse made you an amazing cup of coffee. I mean, sure the local coffee shop across from your office tasted better, but you felt loved that your spouse made it for you. On your way to work, your favorite song came on the radio from high school. You turned up the volume and it started taking you back to your high school days. Your drive to work seemed to go great. Driving on the freeway, a person tried to cut you off but it didn't seem to bother you on this day. You figured that they must have been in a hurry. Today was such a positive and happy day.

Now think about how this day could have been different. You woke up annoyed from the sounds of the birds outside. You thought to yourself, why are the birds so loud this morning. Your spouse made you coffee but it didn't taste as good as the coffee that you usually buy at the local coffee shop. On your way to work, a song came on from high school, and you thought to yourself how did my life end up like this? Memories came back to you on how hard high school was and then a car tried to cut you off on the freeway which made you very upset. You screamed while driving that people like that shouldn't be in such a hurry on the freeway that early in the morning. Your negative thoughts brought you a negative day.

What changed? You did. In the first example you woke up with a positive attitude and didn't let anything bother you. You felt grateful for the birds chirping. You felt loved by your spouse. Listening to music from your high school days made you feel proud and in a lot of ways you were almost reliving some of those exciting memories just by listening to that favorite song. The person that tried to cut you off on the freeway didn't get to you because you just thought to yourself that they must have been in more of a hurry then you. This is how Law of Attraction works. Your positive thoughts attracted a more positive day.

Law of Attraction works on the basic concept that our thoughts and feelings can change our reality. To win contests using Law of Attraction you have to attract winning contests to your life. To do that, you must have a positive mind set. You must focus on positive thoughts about winning. For example, if an athlete had a race the following day, do you think they are thinking that they are going to lose the race? Of course not, the runner is going to have a positive mind thinking that they will win the race.

Do you know anybody that has won the lottery? Do you know anybody that has won the lottery several times or maybe claims that he always wins at casinos? Both are great examples. Because they are already thinking they are going to win the lottery or end up winning at the casino. They attracted winning using Law of Attraction. To win contests, you have to have positive thoughts that you will win the contest even before you do win!

Think

Positive

Gratitude is Everything

Gratitude is a key element in Law of Attraction. Gratitude is being thankful for everything. It's enjoying the simple pleasures and being grateful for everything that is in your life. To truly take advantage of Law of Attraction, you must start your day feeling blessed.

I understand that sometimes this will be a challenge for some of you. For example, maybe you woke up to your kids fighting, or maybe a loud noise outside woke you up. Imagine waking up with a gratitude for life. Feel blessed that you have amazing children to listen to you (most of the time) and even thankful that you can hear that loud noise. Imagine what it must be like to people who can't hear. I bet you if they could hear that noise that woke you up, they would feel so grateful.

When I take my kids to school in the morning, I look around and put myself in a mindset of feeling gratitude for everything that I have. Even when I walk my kids to my car to take them to school, I usually look up to the sky and thank the Universe for everything that I have. I believe Law of Attraction responds to people that are in a state of gratitude. You will need to train your mind to start being thankful for everything you have and what you are going to receive. When I started focusing more on having a grateful state of mind, the amount of contests that I was winning almost doubled to once per week.

Be

Thankful

Exercise 7

What are you grateful for today? List something on each line that you are grateful for today. This can include your family, friends, the house you live in, food, that you have a job, etc.

I am grateful for...

_____

_____

_____

_____

_____

_____

_____

_____

_____

_____

_____

_____

_____

_____

The Fifth Step

The fifth step of How to Use Law of Attraction to Win Contests is to expect that you won the contest before the winner is announced. You have to know 100% that you will win the contest for that specific giveaway and expect it to be given to you by the Universe.

Did you ever apply for a job that you really were excited to work for? So you applied and then they called you for an interview. The interview went really well and you felt like it would be a perfect job for you. When you got back into your car, you knew that that job was yours. You expected to receive that job because it was so perfect. The hours were great; it was something that you really wanted to do. Then the company called you with a job offer.

Now you have to apply the same into Law of Attraction to win contests. You have to expect to win it before it happens. When I started doing this, it was a challenge for me to expect to win something that I just entered. But over time, it will get easier and easier for you to expect to win something before it happens.

Expect

To

Win

Exercise 8

To help you learn to expect that you will win a specific contest, you have to believe it. The best way to expect that you will win is to repeat it over and over again. Writing it down over and over will help.

I expect to win…

_____

_____

_____

_____

_____

_____

_____

_____

_____

_____

_____

_____

_____

_____

_____

_____

_____

The Waiting Game

Lastly, you have to wait until they announce that you are the winner. It's been my experience that sometimes the larger prizes take a while before they are announced. (This might be due to the company hiring an outside company to select the winner.) I have won contests that took weeks to almost a month after the contest ends to receive affirmation of a win. I also have won several contests where they announced the winner the very next day.

I love getting those emails, messages, mail, or even phone calls saying that I was the winner of a contest. It's exciting to know that I won something. But sometimes you do have to wait weeks or even a month or so before they select or announce the winner. All I can say is to be patient and act like you already won the contest. The Law of Attraction is on your side. You will win the contest if you followed these guidelines.

The Sixth Step

The sixth step of How to Use Law of Attraction to Win Contests is to wait till they announce that you are the winner. The smaller prize contests announce winners within a few days after the contest ends. The larger contests could take a few weeks or even several months. The key to this step is to be patient and enjoy winning more contests using this system.

Congratulations

You have completed the last step in this guide. You now have the ability to use Law of Attraction to Win Contests and make all of your dreams come true.

Quick Reference Guide

How to Use Law of Attraction to Win Contests

Step 1:

Decide on what you want to win or is it a current contest being promoted.

Step 2:

Search for a contest that's giving away what you want to win and enter. Or enter if it's a contest that is already being offered.

Step 3:

Ask the Universe to win a specific contest.

Step 4:

Believe that you will win the contest. You need to combine feelings and thought into this process. Visualize yourself winning a contest. Using a vision board helps with the visualizing process but isn't needed to win. Spend a few minutes per day, multiple times per day for the best success.

Step 5:

Expect to win the contest or receive the prize

Step 6:

Now you just have to wait till they announce that you are the winner. The smaller contests announce winners within a day or two after the contest ends. The larger contests could take a few weeks. Be patient. And enjoy winning more contests using this system.

About The Author

Steven R Scott

Steven is a business and computer software instructor. He earned an MBA in Marketing from Regis University, CO and a BS in Business Administration from Bloomsburg University, Bloomsburg, PA.

He "discovered" Law of Attraction in early 2015 and since has manifested over 50 thoughts including moving, jobs, income, debt, winning contests almost every week, and much more. Steven lives with his wife Tara, and their three children Steven, Kevin, and Chris in Middletown, PA. Feel free to contact him at StevenScottMBA@yahoo.com

Coming Soon

The Universe Wants You to Be Happy

Do you really think the Universe wants us to live stressed out about money, jobs, bills, and even with each other? This book will explain in full detail how the Universe wants us to live a fun and fulfilled life while we are here together on Earth and how you can live a happy and balanced life.

Expected Published Date: June 2017

FREE Law of Attraction Newsletter
"IN THE VORTEX"
Success Stories, Inspirational Quotes, Video Clips & Interviews.
Sign up at
InTheVortexNews.com

Made in the USA
Lexington, KY
24 June 2016